MARK KNOPFLER

Strings of Genius - The Life, Legacy, and Music of a Guitar Legend

SCOTT RODMAN

Copyright @ 2024 By Scott Rodman

All rights reserved. No part of this book may be reproduced, distributed, or transmitted in any form or by any means, including photocopying, recording, or other electronic or mechanical methods, without the prior written permission of the publisher, except in the case of brief quotations embodied in critical reviews and specific other noncommercial uses permitted by copyright law.

Contents

INTRODUCTION
    The Man Behind the Strings

CHAPTER 1: HUMBLE BEGINNINGS
    Knopfler's early life in Glasgow and Newcastle
    Family influences and childhood passions

CHAPTER 2: THE BIRTH OF A GUITAR HERO
    Discovering the guitar and early musical inspirations
    The role of folk, blues, and rock in shaping his style

CHAPTER 3: DIRE STRAITS – FROM PUB GIGS TO STARDOM
    The formation of Dire Straits
    Breakthrough albums and iconic songs like "Sultans of Swin."

CHAPTER 4: THE UNIQUE SOUND OF MARK KNOPFLER
    Knopfler's fingerpicking technique and its signature impact

Exploring the fusion of rock, blues, and storytelling in his music

CHAPTER 5: GLOBAL SUCCESS AND CRITICAL ACCLAIM

Dire Straits' global impact and chart-topping albums

The legacy of "Brothers in Arms" and Knopfler's songwriting genius

CHAPTER 6: A SOLO CAREER OF ARTISTIC FREEDOM

Transitioning from Dire Straits to a solo career

Notable albums and collaborations that shaped his post-band career

CHAPTER 7: COMPOSER FOR THE SILVER SCREEN

Knopfler's work in film scores, including "Local Hero" and "The Princess Bride"

How cinematic composition deepened his musical expression

CHAPTER 8: COLLABORATIONS WITH LEGENDS

Working with artists like Bob Dylan, Eric Clapton, and Emmylou Harris

How these collaborations influenced his musical evolution

CHAPTER 9: THE GUITAR COLLECTOR AND ENTHUSIAST

Knopfler's love for vintage guitars and their role in his music

Insights into his most cherished instruments

CHAPTER 10: BEYOND THE STAGE – MARK KNOPFLER'S PERSONAL JOURNEY

Life outside of music: passions, philanthropy, and personal growth

The Legacy of a Guitar Genius

CONCLUSION

Strings That Will Echo Forever

INTRODUCTION

The Man Behind the Strings

Not only is Mark Knopfler a legendary guitarist, but he is also a composer, storyteller, and musical visionary whose name has resonance with listeners of all ages. Mark Knopfler's music is a timeless example of masterful composition in a world of passing trends and sounds. His music exhibits an uncommon genuineness in any era, from the deft fingerpicking that characterizes his guitar skills to the poignant lyrics that capture the subtleties of life.

Although many people only remember Knopfler as the lead singer of Dire Straits, whose songs from the late 20th century included "Money for Nothing" and "Sultans of Swing," his contributions to music go far beyond the realm of top-charting rock tunes. Throughout his over 50-year career, he has continuously changed and experimented with different genres, explored songwriting as a narrative means, and worked with some of the most excellent musicians of all time.

Not only is Mark Knopfler's technical skill unmatched by other guitar giants, but guitarists worldwide admire his unique fingerstyle technique. He can render human experience into music, eloquently expressing the grand narratives and the tiny, private moments of existence. Knopfler's writing always feels very personal, whether he's narrating stories of faraway places and lost loves or writing about the typical lives of regular people.

Unmistakably rich, warm, and incredibly complex is Knopfler's sound. His tunes frequently lack needless flare, concentrating instead on the unadulterated emotional essence of the song. Because of his exceptional ability to conjure images through his lyrics and his economy of sound, he has established himself as one of his generation's most profound and well-respected artists. Knopfler's genius is in his restraint, unlike many of his contemporaries who may rely on bombast and spectacle. His solos entice you gently, exposing their beauty and depth little by bit rather than grabbing your attention outright.

Knopfler's accomplishments, however, extend beyond the guitar. He has written stories as a songwriter that go beyond the parameters of a conventional pop or rock tune. He finds inspiration in history, literature, and his surroundings. His songs frequently have the colorful, multi-layered, and vibrant quality of short stories set to music. His songs vividly depict the settings and people that make up his world while touching on universal themes of loss, longing, and discovery.

Knopfler has collaborated with a wide range of musicians throughout the years, including Tina Turner, Eric Clapton, Bob Dylan, and Chet Atkins. While every partnership has added something fresh to his music, he has never wavered in his unique voice or aesthetic. Knopfler's artistic curiosity knows no bounds, as evidenced by his work producing soundtracks for legendary movies like *Local Hero* and *The Princess

Bride* or his release of solo albums exploring folk, blues, and roots music.

For Knopfler, music extends who he is, not just his job. He approaches his career with the humility and commitment of a craftsman, constantly looking to improve his abilities and elevate his artistic expression. Even while his reserved demeanor doesn't fit the stereotypical idea of a rock star, that makes him so alluring. In an industry where ostentation and ego are common, Knopfler has remained loyal to the music, allowing his talent to speak for itself.

This book is more than just an homage to his accomplishments or a list of his albums and awards. This is an investigation into the person behind the music—what motivates and inspires him, and how he has maintained a career characterized by financial success and artistic integrity. We will explore every facet of Mark Knopfler's incredible journey by delving into his catalog, conducting in-depth interviews, and exploring old materials. This book will provide a window into the life and legacy of a guitar great, from his early days navigating the challenges of a young artist to his ascension to become one of the most revered personalities in music.

Even though Mark Knopfler doesn't chase attention, his contributions to the music industry are undeniable. One thing becomes evident as we travel through his life: his legacy extends beyond the notes he plays and encompasses the stories he tells and the human connections his music makes with listeners. This is the tale of a man who, in ways few could have predicted, changed the sound of modern music through quiet tenacity and unwavering passion.

CHAPTER 1: HUMBLE BEGINNINGS

Knopfler's early life in Glasgow and Newcastle

The early years of Mark Knopfler's life are spent in Glasgow, Scotland, a post-war metropolis still recovering from the devastation of war and molded by its industrial background. Though he was born on August 12, 1949, in a time of societal unrest, his family's tale held great significance in and of itself. In the 1930s, his father, Erwin Knopfler, was a Jewish architect from Hungary who came to Britain to avoid the growing horrors of Nazism. For the Knopfler family, that experience of survival through displacement was irrevocably changed. His mother, Louisa Mary, was a northeastern English teacher who instilled in her children a spirit of intellectual discipline and inquiry.

Sharp differences in city life shaped Mark's early years in Glasgow. In the 1950s, Glasgow was a vibrant city full of tenacity and resiliency, but it was also a place where people were very loyal to their heritage. From a young age, Mark's perspective would be shaped by this dichotomy of adversity combined with perseverance. The Knopfler family did not lead an abundant life by any means. Despite being well-educated and morally upright, his parents had modest lives and instilled in their kids the importance of diligence and tenacity. Mark grew up surrounded by a blend of cultures and experiences, which would later impact his varied musical pallet.

A turning point came when the Knopfler family relocated to Newcastle-upon-Tyne, a northeastern English city, when he was seven. It was more than just a simple relocation—the relocation involved a shift in mood. Glasgow was one thing; Newcastle, with its deep industrial origins, was another. Newcastle was a working-class town strongly influenced by the shipbuilding and coal mining sectors. Its residents had a unique identity characterized by pride, resiliency, and groundedness.

Newcastle became a defining experience for Mark, influencing not just his music but also his whole persona. He was captivated by the people's directness, sense of belonging, and sense of pride in the area. For Mark, these locations were more than simply places; they were a trove of narratives and personalities that would eventually find their way into his songs. Despite his youth, he had a keen sense of his surroundings, and it was from these that the roots of his artistic expression were first planted.

His life had been influenced by music, but it had yet to take center stage. His early introduction to the arts came from his mother's love of the piano and classical music. But blues, folk, and rock 'n' roll from Glasgow and Newcastle's cultural melting pot started to permeate his mind. In these formative years, there was no pivotal moment when music claimed him, but the components were all there, just waiting to come together.

Mark went to Gosforth Grammar School in Newcastle, where he was a standout student in English and other disciplines and showed an early interest in storytelling, which would later define him. But he wasn't the boisterous or cocky kind; instead, he liked to watch, listen, and take in everything around him. His early schooling prepared him for the narrative-driven approach he would take to songwriting, although it was a more subdued interest then and didn't foreshadow a music career.

While living in Newcastle, Mark was surrounded by the noises of a changing Britain. The radio evolved into a friend and a doorway to other realms. He first heard artists like Hank Marvin and The Shadows through this window, and their sound sparked something within him. Young Mark connected with the complex guitar technique and the emotional range of Marvin's performance. At this point, he was far from taking up a guitar, but it was a language he felt obliged to comprehend.

The Newcastle Knopfler family was a clever, intelligent family. His parents stressed the value of education in navigating life and finding a path to a job. This rigorous academic approach, especially from his father's side, established expectations for Mark. It was always about content, not about ostentatious fame or prosperity. This focus on depth would be evident in his subsequent work as he made a name for himself as a reflective artist who talked authentically and wrote meaningful lyrics rather than as a typical rock star.

Britain saw a significant change in its cultural landscape as the 1960s got underway. Mark was captivated by the music, much like many people in his generation were, as a surge of innovative sounds and concepts was introduced with the British Invasion. The Beatles, Rolling Stones, and Bob Dylan—musicians who were more than just performers but cultural icons influencing the very fabric of young identity—filled the airwaves with their revolutionary sounds.

On the other hand, Mark was introduced to the guitar through the more somber facets of the music industry rather than the dominant pop tendencies. It felt more like a quiet finding than a loud revelation when, at the age of 15, he eventually acquired a used guitar. Rather than thinking of himself as destined for fame, he saw the guitar as a personal haven and a means of communicating with a deeper part of himself.

His early guitar playing was more about experimenting with a new kind of storytelling than winning over people or entertaining large audiences. He was becoming increasingly enthralled with blues music, particularly since the genre's emotional profundity and simplicity resonated with him. During these formative years, he learned to play the guitar by ear, practicing in silence and frequently by himself while taking in the tones of legendary guitarists like B.B. King and Django Reinhardt. His fingerpicking style, which would eventually characterize his sound, gradually developed due to many hours spent determining what was most comfortable for him.

Mark's youth in Newcastle was characterized by quiet devotion and investigation. Although he wasn't quite a musician in the conventional sense, the groundwork was being done. These were years of self-examination and introspection, of taking in the gritty working-class Newcastle and the broader cultural shifts throughout Britain. Though not very noteworthy, this time in Mark Knopfler's life helped to shape both the man and the artist he would become.

Family influences and childhood passions

Mark Knopfler's early inspirations came from his family, who shaped his interests long before he became well-known as a great guitarist and songwriter. In his early years, Erwin Knopfler, his father, loomed large. Erwin was a Jewish émigré from Hungary who escaped the Nazis before World War II. He had a history of intellectual grit and survival. As an architect, he emphasized accuracy, diligence, and the discipline of producing something long-lasting—qualities that would recur in Mark's professional life. Even though his father didn't talk much about the more difficult times during his flight from fascism, Mark felt the weight of that past in a subtle but significant way. It instilled in him a sense of the transience of life and the value of creating something meaningful out of whatever resources life throws at you, be they chords and melodies or bricks and masonry.

In a different way, but no less powerful, was his mother, Louisa Mary. She instilled in the Knopfler family a passion for education and an appreciation for culture during her tenure as a schoolteacher. Her first exposure to the power of music encouraged Mark and his brother David to follow their interests by listening to classical CDs. Louisa's parenting has an intellectual element, albeit not in the literal sense of encouraging her kids to thrive academically. Instead, it was about cultivating an attitude of inquiry and learning. Mark cultivated a quiet enthusiasm for storytelling in this supportive setting, which would eventually become essential to his music.

He grew up surrounded by talk, music, and books. His parents were voracious readers, and there was a vast array of books in their house, from poetry to political philosophy. Despite being relatively short, his early years in Glasgow were influential since they exposed him to various viewpoints. Growing up in a home where history was a constant presence, Mark keenly understood the significance of narrative—how people's lives, including his own family, are influenced by more powerful forces. His father's experiences as a refugee escaping authoritarianism gave him a sense that personal stories may be spectacular, even when lived quietly.

Mark was utterly engrossed in the world of sounds and stories, although many kids would have preferred to concentrate only on playing. Classical music in the family provided Mark with a basis for comprehending structure and form in composition, even though he never became skilled on the piano due to his mother's love of music. Before long, music in the Knopfler home transcended its role as background noise. It gradually permeated Mark's early life, gently forming his identity.

Another meaningful relationship he had was with his brother, David. Many of his passions were also shared by David, who would go on to join him in Dire Straits. Their love of music and stories solidified their brother bond. In a home where discussions about literature, history, or the status of the world frequently occurred, the two brothers found comfort in music as a means of self-expression. Their shared experiences in the family home during these early years saw them form an unspoken bond, even if their paths would subsequently diverge.

His early interests extended beyond music. He was curious about everything and particularly interested in literature, sports, and the arts. He did exceptionally well in school, especially in English, and it became evident that he had a natural talent for storytelling—not just in written form but also in music. Teachers saw his talent early on; he was especially good at writing well-thought-out and intricately detailed narratives. Writing, like music, allowed Mark to build worlds and tell stories that felt both personal and universal, so it wasn't simply about earning excellent grades.

But Mark had many passions, whereas many kids might concentrate on just one. One of them was football. Growing up in the working-class surroundings of Newcastle after his family's transfer, football was more than simply a sport—it was a cultural institution, a means to connect with the community. Even though he felt he wasn't meant to pursue this as a career, Mark enthusiastically played the game. But even after giving up his football boots for a guitar, he carried the lessons of discipline, collaboration, and belonging he experienced on the pitch.

The sea also held a fascination for some. Living close to the River Tyne and observing the large ships come and go from Newcastle's port gave Mark a quiet passion for the sea that he eventually incorporated into his music.

The picture of the sea, of long travels, of ports and sailors, would subsequently become regular themes in his songs. These early impressions would come to life in songs like "Sailing to Philadelphia," demonstrating how deeply ingrained those early influences had become.

Young Mark's experiences were shaped by a complex interplay of factors, including his brother's company, his mother's passion for culture, his father's past, and Newcastle's working-class environment. These factors provided him with a basis for his worldview and for his music. These were not lessons learned in a classroom or from a textbook but from his upbringing, his family's stories, and his daily experiences.

CHAPTER 2: THE BIRTH OF A GUITAR HERO

Discovering the guitar and early musical inspirations

Instead of a sudden, spectacular epiphany, Mark Knopfler's discovery of the guitar was the product of a slow, almost silent awakening. Although music was always present in the Knopfler home growing up, it wasn't the dominating influence one might anticipate in the formative years of a future guitar hero. His mother's library of classical music laid a foundation, but Mark only started to realize the guitar's allure once he was a teenager.

The radio was an odd source of inspiration for this new love. It was the mid-1960s, and Britain was in the midst of a cultural revolution, with rock and roll exploding onto the scene and transforming the landscape of popular music. However, Mark's pivotal moments were neither The Rolling Stones' ascent nor Beatlemania's eruption. On the contrary, hearing Hank Marvin of The Shadows triggered something inside of him. Marvin's crisp, catchy guitar lines made him sound like he was telling a tale with sound, and Mark was drawn to the concept of using an instrument to communicate.

Mark was struck not only by Marvin's technical skill but also by the clarity of his emotions in his performance. His use of the tremolo arm and his ability to shape and bend notes all felt like something incredibly personal. This expression resonated with Mark in a manner he hadn't experienced before. It was more than simply the music; it was also about the emotion that went into it. That playing immediately spoke to Mark and served as the first significant source of inspiration for his budding musical career.

At first, though, he had difficulty getting to the guitar. Growing up in a working-class household, I was not afforded the luxury of purchasing instruments impulsively. Mark's first guitar was a cheap, used instrument that could have been more playable by most people's standards. But to Mark, it was the key to unlocking a new world. Its flaws didn't stop him; they strengthened his resolve to get it to sing. He started teaching himself how to play by experimenting with various sounds and learning by ear. Even though it was frustrating at times, this trial-and-error method helped him naturally establish his style. He didn't receive official instruction, which could have helped him because it freed him from the limitations of conventional methods and allowed him to explore the guitar.

Mark had a wide range of influences in his early years. He found himself pulling more and more to the blues in addition to British rock and roll culture. Significant figures in his life included musicians like Lonnie Johnson, Muddy Waters, and B.B. King. Mark was drawn to the blues' unadulterated emotion and simplicity, and he was amazed at how much could be expressed with so few notes. Mark was drawn to the raw honesty and edge of the blues, which set them apart from the more refined rock and roll sound emerging from the UK at the time. He listened to these recordings for hours, trying to analyze the minute details of the musicians' performances and internalizing the blues language in the process.

Another influential person in Mark's early musical life was Bob Dylan. Mark had never experienced narrative and musicianship quite like he did with Dylan. It was about painting a picture, encapsulating a whole scene or emotion in a few lines, not just about catchy tunes or virtuoso guitar work. Starting to compose music, Mark discovered an outlet for his love of English and narrative from his school days, and this kind of depth spoke to him.

Even while Mark had grown to love the guitar by the time he was in his late teens, he had not yet considered playing it as a career. His music was less driven by a desire for fame or wealth and more by inner fulfillment. He would spend hours in his room honing his fingerpicking skills and developing his ability to blend rhythm and melody, a talent that would eventually come to define him. For Mark, this procedure was contemplative. He was motivated by the excitement of learning new things and pushing the boundaries of his instrument, not by the need to impress others or prove himself.

Mark also started exploring songwriting during this time. His passion had always been storytelling; he found he could convey stories in novel ways with the guitar. Although his early songs lacked complexity, they set the stage for the subsequent career-defining combination of musicianship and storytelling. Mark was influenced by Dylan and his favorite blues musicians, and he started to view music as a means of communication that allowed people to express concepts, feelings, and experiences that were beyond words.

Not too long after, his love of music started to seep into the public domain from his private practice sessions. He began performing in neighborhood bands in Newcastle, covering hits from the time while progressively developing his material. Although these early performances were not glamorous, they were crucial in helping him build his confidence and execute to the best of his abilities. Even in smaller settings with fewer patrons, he continued to perform live because he enjoyed the rush of engaging with an audience via his guitar.

Early in his guitar adventure, Mark wasn't concerned about getting significant results or feeling good immediately. It was a gradual process of growing, learning, and listening. The fusion of American blues, British rock, and folk storytelling that shaped him would be the cornerstone of his musical career. These early influences influenced not only his manner of playing but also his conception of music as an art form, emphasizing sincerity, skill, and the potency of a powerful narrative.

By the time he was ready to take the stage, Mark Knopfler's relationship with the guitar had evolved from a childhood infatuation into something far more substantial: a lifetime dedication to both the instrument and the art of music-making.

The role of folk, blues, and rock in shaping his style

Rock, folk, and blues are frequently used to characterize Mark Knopfler's musical style, with each genre influencing his approach to the guitar and lyrics differently. These genres were the foundation of his musical identity, not just some passing fancy. From the start, Knopfler was drawn to the intensity of rock, the storytelling quality of folk, and the authenticity and emotional depth of blues, each of which contributed a unique element to his developing style.

Knopfler was significantly influenced early on by the blues in particular. As a teenager, he was enthralled with the unadulterated passion exhibited by musicians such as B.B. King, Muddy Waters, and Robert Johnson. What attracted him to the blues wasn't only the technical talent of the guitarists but the way they could create tremendous emotions with minimalism. The simplicity with which the blues could convey happiness, sadness, or longing with a few notes made them so beautiful. The way the blues guitarists employed space in their playing, allowing the listener's imagination to fill in the blanks, captivated Knopfler. The idea that "less is more" became a defining feature of Knopfler's performance. He was more concerned with playing with feeling and allowing the song to breathe than he was with technical flair or dazzling solos.

However, Knopfler was inspired by the tales that accompanied the songs, more than just the blues' sound. Blues music frequently conveyed stories of adversity, tenacity, and survival—themes that struck a chord with Knopfler personally. He was drawn to the blues' storytelling element as much as its musical quality, and his songwriting would thereafter be distinguished by this narrative focus. In addition to moving listeners with their sound, he intended his songs to engage listeners with the narratives they conveyed. This is when folk music came into play.

The rich storytelling history of folk music had a significant impact on Knopfler's sound as well. He learned from musicians like Woody Guthrie and Bob Dylan that a song could be more than just a pleasant melody and a means of delving into intricate concepts, feelings, and characters. Folk's concentration on lyrics and narrative structure captivated the part of Knopfler, that enjoyed writing and storytelling. Folk offered him the structure for his lyrics, while blues gave him the emotional basis for his music. Folk taught Knopfler the value of a well-written narrative, and this idea has since informed much of his music.

In particular, Bob Dylan rose to prominence in Knopfler's musical universe. Knopfler greatly admired Dylan's ability to incorporate complex narratives into his songs. Dylan didn't merely write songs about love or heartache; he also built entire worlds with vibrant characters and breathtaking scenery. Knopfler was deeply affected by this narrative complexity, and he started to view his songs as narratives having a beginning, middle, and finish rather than merely emotional emotions. This was reflected in Knopfler's songwriting, as he started composing intricately lyrically and musically.

Knopfler's music was emotionally and narratively grounded in blues and folk. Still, rock offered him the opportunity to combine those components in a more dynamic way. With musicians like The Beatles, The Rolling Stones, and Eric Clapton stretching the definition of what rock might be, the 1960s and 1970s were thrilling moments for rock music. For Knopfler, rock stood for freedom: combining many genres, trying out novel tones, and connecting with a larger audience.

Even while Knopfler never adopted the flashy, loud guitar solos that were fashionable in rock at the time, he did infuse his playing with the spirit and enthusiasm of the genre. In many respects, his approach to rock was a synthesis of the storytelling sensibility he received from folk music and the restraint he learned from the blues. Because of this combination, he produced a sound all his own: a rock-based blend of nuance, passion, and narrative depth.

Dire Straits, Mark Knopfler's breakout band, was the perfect example of this fusion of styles. In contrast to the more flamboyant rock groups of the late 1970s, their sound was more straightforward and focused on melody, groove, and poetic storytelling. "Sultans of Swing," the band's first song, is a prime illustration of how Knopfler combined many genres to create something original and new. Though the song's complex fingerpicking style and observational lyrics are based on folk and blues traditions, the song's driving beat and guitar work are unmistakably rock. It was a song that looked to the future while borrowing inspiration from the past and feeling familiar and fresh.

Although Knopfler's musical style changed throughout the years, his underlying influences stayed the same. *Brothers in Arms* and other albums showed how well he could combine rock, blues, and folk to create a single, unified sound. His ability to write songs that were not just musically captivating but also full of emotional and narrative detail was demonstrated by songs like "Romeo and Juliet." The song's sad guitar lines are a tribute to the blues, and the folktale-inspired lyrics convey a timeless tale of love and sorrow.

Knopfler's style has stayed loyal to the aspects that influenced him as a budding musician, even in his subsequent solo work. His albums are full of songs more akin to musical short stories, with every note and phrase having a distinct purpose. Knopfler's music is still a tribute to the genres that shaped him, whether he uses the energy of rock, the melancholy of the blues, or the folk narrative.

CHAPTER 3: DIRE STRAITS – FROM PUB GIGS TO STARDOM

The formation of Dire Straits

Mark Knopfler saw the founding of Dire Straits in 1977 as a turning point in his career and in the development of rock music. Knopfler was slightly older than most up-and-coming rock performers at the time, having already been in his late 20s. He had been practicing for years, playing in several bands and balancing work as a journalist and teacher. But even though he loved music, forming a band only took shape once he got in touch with his brother, David Knopfler.

His family and his musical career have always been closely entwined, and this relationship was crucial to the formation of Dire Straits. David, who was also a songwriter and musician, was inspired by his brother's love of music. Mark's deft fingerpicking and David's rhythmic playing, combined with their frequent jam sessions, produced a sound that was basic, new, and distinct from the popular rock of the time. The idea for Dire Straits was ignited at one of these meetings in their compact Deptford, South London municipal apartment.

The band's original members were Pick Withers on drums, John Illsley on bass, and Mark and David. Illsley and Withers were both accomplished musicians, and their straightforward approach to rhythm created the ideal framework for the guitars played by the Knopfler brothers. In particular, Illsley played a significant role in the band's early development. He was a Deptford resident who became friends with Mark because they both loved music and wanted to make something other than the flashy, overly processed rock that was playing on the radio.

The band's early rehearsals were unassuming. Their practice sessions were held in small, inexpensive places and lacked considerable equipment. However, their creativity and focus more than made up for their need for more resources. The intention was always clear: to produce music that was simple and uncomplicated, emphasizing musicianship and storytelling over the loud, flashy theatrics that had gained popularity in the late 1970s.

The band's sound started to take shape throughout these practices. Mark's fingerpicking approach, influenced by his love for folk and blues, was notable. Knopfler played with clarity, melody, and understatement, unlike many other guitarists of the day who were drawn to distortion and power chords. His songs offered stories—tales of everyday people, street artists, and struggling musicians—which stood in stark contrast to the excesses of stadium rock. Dire Straits grew to be known for its simplicity.

The band's name also alluded to its predicament. A friend of Withers proposed the song "Dire Straits" as a reference to the financial struggles the band members were going through at the time. They were literally in desperate circumstances, living on a shoestring budget. The band stands out from the crowd despite its limited resources thanks to its close-knit chemistry and distinctive sound.

Their big break came when they recorded a few songs on a demo cassette, one of which was "Sultans of Swing." Charlie Gillett, a prominent DJ on BBC Radio London, became interested in the song due to its catchy rhythm, unique guitar work, and vivid lyrics about a local jazz band performing in an almost empty pub. Gillett aired the track on his show, and the response was instant. Dire Straits' clean, uncomplicated sound drew listeners in, and Phonogram Records soon awarded the band a recording contract.

Dire Straits released their debut album of the same name in 1978. The popularity of "Sultans of Swing" played a major role in its rapid rise in the US and Europe, despite its initial lack of notice in the UK. The song became a global hit, launching the group into stardom and presenting Mark Knopfler as a new breed of guitar hero—one who relied more on dexterity and finesse than on distortion or flashy solos.

Breakthrough albums and iconic songs like "Sultans of Swin."

Mark Knopfler's unique style and storytelling prowess were evident in a string of breakthrough albums and hit songs that propelled Dire Straits' explosive rise to prominence. The band's 1978 self-titled first album, which presented listeners with a sound that was both new and genuine, was a turning point in their career. But their 1979 release of Communiqué, their second album, cemented their place as a prominent force in the rock world.

"Sultans of Swing," which perfectly captured the band's spirit, was undoubtedly the album's best track. Knopfler penned a song about a local band performing in an almost empty pub to capture the essence of musicians who play for the love of music rather than fame or wealth. The lyrics vividly depicted the incident, discussing the pleasures and challenges of being a professional musician. The song's catchy melody and delicate fingerpicking guitar performance by Knopfler connected with listeners, propelling it to commercial success.

In addition to being a big hit in the UK, "Sultans of Swing" also became quite popular in the US, topping the charts there. The song's success was astounding, especially considering how far it deviated from the late 1970s rock scene's prevalent patterns. Dire Straits offered a more understated and nuanced style, whereas many bands embraced bombastic sounds and lavish productions. The band stands out thanks to Knopfler's crisp guitar tone and tight, simple arrangements, which garnered praise from critics and a devoted following.

Following the success of their debut, Dire Straits released *Communiqué* in June 1979. Despite not being as successful commercially as its predecessor, the album had many standout tracks that enhanced the band's rising stardom. Songs like "Once Upon a Time in the West" and "Lady Writer" demonstrated Knopfler's talent for narrative, fusing realistic topics with vivid imagery. The album hinted at the band's impending change while preserving their distinctive sound and broadening their musical pallet.

Dire Straits found their footing by publishing their third album, *Making Movies*, in 1980. A significant turning point in the band's career was the record, both creatively and commercially. One of the best songs, "Tunnel of Love," stood out for its opulent sound and romantic themes. "Romeo and Juliet," a moving story of love and longing that became one of the band's most lasting masterpieces, was also included on this album. With its eerie tune and stirring lyrics, the song showcased Knopfler's skill at fusing intimate storytelling with more universal issues, forging a profoundly meaningful connection with the audience.

In addition to being produced differently from other albums, Knopfler's Making Movies record featured a collaboration with renowned producer Jimmy Iovine. The end result was a refined sound that preserved the band's essential qualities while giving the song more depth. Dire Straits gained notoriety and recognition for their hard work and emotional openness, which elevated them to the top of the rock music hierarchy.

Brothers in Arms, Dire Straits' follow-up album, was released in 1985 and would eventually come to define their legacy. The album became a global multi-platinum success and produced multiple hit songs, including "Brothers in Arms," the title track. The song, which showcased rich orchestration and heartbreaking lyrics, delves into themes of loss and struggle, solidifying Knopfler's reputation as a master storyteller.

"Money for Nothing," one of the band's most well-known tracks, was another excellent track on the album. It became a cultural hit thanks to its brilliant music video, memorable guitar riff, and scathing critique of the music business. Along with topping the charts, the song was recognized with a Grammy Award for Best Rock Performance by a Duo or Group.

Dire Straits cemented their legacy in rock history with *Brothers in Arms*, and Knopfler's distinctive guitar style and compositions continued to impact a new wave of performers. The album's popularity demonstrated the band's ability to write songs that connected with listeners on several levels while maintaining artistic integrity.

Dire Straits released several albums during their career that demonstrated how their sound and thematic depth were developing. The 1991 album On Every Street included songs like "Calling Elvis" and "Heavy Fuel," which further showcased Knopfler's skill as a songwriter. The band's commercial zenith had passed, but its music was still relevant and significant.

CHAPTER 4: THE UNIQUE SOUND OF MARK KNOPFLER

Knopfler's fingerpicking technique and its signature impact

One of the things that most defines Mark Knopfler's musical style is his fingerpicking technique, which has left a lasting impression on the guitar community. He differs from many of his peers who frequently preferred a more conventional use of picks or plectrums with this unusual approach. Because Knopfler prefers to play without a pick, his guitar work is instantly recognizable due to the level of nuance and expressiveness he can express.

A variety of musical genres influenced Knopfler during his early years, including folk, blues, and country music, which helped him on his path to becoming a proficient fingerpicker. Fingerpicking methods abound in many genres, and as he honed his craft, he acquired their subtleties. Fingerstyle guitarists like Chet Atkins and Jerry Reed taught Knopfler how to blend complex melodies with steady rhythmic backing. His style is distinguished by a deft use of melody and harmony, frequently incorporating fluid changes from chordal sections to plucked notes.

In numerous Dire Straits tracks, Knopfler's fingerpicking is audible. Tracks like "Sultans of Swing" exhibit his ability to weave complicated rhythms that create a beautiful sound tapestry. The song's complex guitar lines are percussion-heavy and melodic, giving it a solid rhythmic foundation. While Knopfler's fingers deftly slide over the higher strings, his thumb provides a stable foundation for the bottom notes, resulting in a rich, dynamic sound. Using this method, he can add a texture to his music that is difficult to accomplish with a pick and use his playing to express various emotions.

His fingerpicking style is versatile, evidenced by tunes like "Romeo and Juliet." The delicate fingerstyle guitar riff that opens the song creates a contemplative atmosphere that goes well with the moving lyrics. The strength of Knopfler's technique is demonstrated by his ability to convey vulnerability and longing through his guitar playing. Listeners are drawn in by the subtleties of his playing, which range from the careful plucking of each string to the gentle touch of his fingers.

Furthermore, Knopfler's fingerpicking style has affected many guitarists from various genres. Musicians respect his expressive playing as much as the technical prowess needed to carry out such complex rhythms. Many wannabe guitarists have tried to imitate Knopfler's approach by adding fingerpicking to their song lists. His method has rekindled interest in fingerstyle playing and encouraged a new wave of players to investigate the potential of this style.

Knopfler's fingerpicking is essential not only for its technical qualities but also for the sound it makes. His usage of light gauge strings produces a clear, bright tone that fits his style. His fingerpicking style and equipment selection combine to create his work's distinctive sound. His tasteful collection of guitars, which includes Gibson Les Pauls and Fender Stratocasters, further expands his range of tones and enables him to produce a wide range of tones, from lively and exuberant to sad and reflective.

Another noticeable characteristic of Knopfler's fingerpicking is his use of dynamics. He frequently uses changes in assault and volume to give his tunes an ebb and flow. Using this dynamic range, he can create tension and release, engrossing listeners in the emotional terrain of his song. His skill in playing can arouse sentiments of joy, longing, and nostalgia, demonstrating his capacity to engage his listeners on a deeper level.

Knopfler's fingerpicking approach is not merely a way of playing the guitar but an extension of his musical personality. His method reflects a storytelling style in which each note and phrase advances the song's story. This can also be heard in his solo work, as he stays loyal to his hallmark style while continuing to explore new musical horizons.

Exploring the fusion of rock, blues, and storytelling in his music

Mark Knopfler's music is a rich tapestry woven from the threads of rock, blues, and storytelling, creating a distinctive and compelling sound. This fusion demonstrates his incredible storytelling and composing skills and his technical mastery as a guitarist. Knopfler has made a name for himself in the music industry through his compositions and lyrics. His songs all tell compelling stories that connect with listeners.

The rock genre laid the groundwork for Knopfler's musical career by emphasizing strong riffs and upbeat live performances. But he added blues music's raw passion and emotional depth to his rock style. His use of expressive vibrato and note bending to portray emotion in his guitar playing is a clear example of the blues' impact. The combination of bluesy guitar lines and lively rock rhythms in songs like "Walk of Life" results in a joyful yet melancholic ambiance. How different genres interact in Knopfler's music reflects his aim to establish a musical and emotional connection with his listeners.

The most distinctive aspect of Knopfler's songwriting is his ability to narrate stories. He creates stories that take listeners to new locations and eras by drawing on both his own and other people's experiences. His songs frequently have familiar characters and vivid imagery, which makes it easy for listeners to become lost in the tales he narrates. In "Telegraph Road," for example, Knopfler explores themes of ambition, change, and loss while telling the story of a man's life and highway construction. The song's length and intricacy reflect life's journey, with melodic changes corresponding to the story's ebb and flow.

Knopfler typically incorporates cultural and historical allusions into his storytelling rock and blues compositions to give his songs a deeper meaning. Songs like "Brothers in Arms" address issues of brotherhood and battle, relying on individual and group histories to provide a moving meditation on human existence. The song evokes empathy and understanding in listeners with its melancholic tune and stirring lyrics. Knopfler can address important subjects by combining several genres while keeping rock music approachable and appealing.

Furthermore, Knopfler's skill in crafting evocative soundscapes enhances his storytelling prowess. In songs like "So Far Away," he uses complex arrangements and understated instrumentation to elicit feelings consistent with the text. The story is enhanced by the soft fingerpicking and melodic embellishments, which help the audience understand the message's significance. This exacting attention to detail in the song's lyrics and melody is a prime example of Knopfler's skillful blending of several musical inspirations to produce a single, cohesive artistic vision.

His solo work further highlights Knopfler's investigation of this confluence. His records, firmly rooted in the rock and blues traditions, exhibit a variety of styles, including *Golden Heart* and *Get Lucky*. For instance, he combines elements of rock with a loose rhythm in "Cleaning My Gun," which makes you feel relaxed while conveying a thought-provoking story. His flexibility as an artist is demonstrated by his ability to transition between genres while keeping a constant voice.

Knopfler's cooperation with other artists, which broadens his musical taste, is another facet of this synthesis. His collaborations with musicians from various genres—including folk, country, and even classical—have enabled him to blend a wide range of inspirations into his style. For instance, he masterfully combines rock and country music elements with Emmylou Harris on "All the Roadrunning" while upholding the storytelling tradition that characterizes his body of work. This spirit of cooperation broadens his musical possibilities and emphasizes how universal his ideas and stories are.

CHAPTER 5: GLOBAL SUCCESS AND CRITICAL ACCLAIM

Dire Straits' global impact and chart-topping albums

Dire Straits emerged as one of the most influential rock bands of the late 20th century, enduringly affecting the music world. The band captured audiences worldwide with their distinct style, blending rock, blues, and country influences. This led to a string of chart-topping albums that cemented the band's legacy.

After forming in 1977, Dire Straits became well-known thanks to their self-titled debut album, which highlighted Mark Knopfler's unique guitar style and poetic storytelling. Hits from the album included "Sultans of Swing," which became an unexpected hit, topping charts across multiple nations and making the band a powerful force in the music industry. Dire Straits's success in the future was made possible by the track's distinctive fusion of catchy guitar riffs and gripping storytelling.

Communiqué(1979), their follow-up album, maintained the momentum and expanded on their distinctive sound. The album demonstrated the band's skill and new direction even if it did not have the same level of commercial success as its predecessor. The band's rising fame was aided by the track "Lady Writer," which had a lot of radio hits.

But Dire Straits *Making Movies* (1980), their third album, catalyzed change. The album, which included the well-known songs "Romeo and Juliet" and "Tunnel of Love," was a commercial and critical success. In particular, "Romeo and Juliet" brought out Knopfler's talent for narrative and emotional range, connecting with audiences and leaving a lasting impression on the rock world. Due to the album's popularity, Dire Straits gained recognition in the music business and started to draw a devoted fan base worldwide.

The band's release of *Love Over Gold* in 1982 helped catapult them into global recognition. One of the album's standout tracks, "Telegraph Road," is a nearly 14-minute musical excursion highlighting Mark Knopfler's deft guitar work and compelling narration. With the album topping charts in multiple countries, Dire Straits's popularity kept rising. The band distinguished itself from its peers by fusing rock with intricate musical arrangements, which made them a singular force in the music industry.

The publication of *Brothers in Arms* (1985), an album that would become one of the best-selling recordings of all time, marked the pinnacle of Dire Straits' career. Among the most well-known tracks on the album were "Money for Nothing" and "Walk of Life." "Money for Nothing," which received the Grammy Award for Best Rock Performance by a Duo or Group, became a massive hit because of its catchy guitar riff and thought-provoking lyrics. The band's international recognition was enhanced by the revolutionary animation in the accompanying music video, which was heavily aired on MTV. The record's flawless production and seamless fusion of pop and rock influences made it famous with listeners and propelled it to multi-platinum success.

Dire Straits became a household brand when *Brothers in Arms* ruled the charts, and their music transcended national boundaries. Several nations, including the US, Canada, and the UK, ranked the album their top. It did well commercially and won praise from critics, enhancing Dire Straits' standing as one of the best rock bands of the day. The album is a timeless masterpiece because of how profoundly fans connected with its themes of struggle and compassion.

Beyond their success on the charts, Dire Straits significantly influenced the sound of rock music in the 1980s. Their openness to trying out other musical genres, such as blues, jazz, and country, impacted many artists who came after them. Knopfler's fingerpicking style and melodic sensitivities influenced a generation of guitarists, and the band's blend of music and narration served as a model for songwriters to come.

Dire Straits' influence persisted even after their original dissolution in 1995. New listener generations still demand their albums, and their music is still praised. The band's original sound has a lasting impact, as evidenced by the work of modern performers in various genres.

The legacy of "Brothers in Arms" and Knopfler's songwriting genius

The 1985 single "Brothers in Arms" is a pillar of both rock music and Mark Knopfler's remarkable career. In addition to being a huge commercial success, this album permanently changed the genre and demonstrated Knopfler's extraordinary songwriting and musicianship.

The film "Brothers in Arms" has received worldwide praise and critical acclaim, highlighting its legacy. Following its release, the album shot to the top of international charts, striking number one in the US, Canada, and the UK, among other nations. It was among the first albums to be issued on CD, and the music industry's benchmark for audio fidelity was raised by its sound quality. *Brothers in Arms* is one of the best-selling albums ever, having sold over 30 million copies worldwide.

The core of "Brothers in Arms" is Knopfler's unmatched songwriting skill, which blends catchy melodies with moving words. "Brothers in Arms," the album's title tune, is a sad ballad considering grief, fraternity, and battle themes. Fingerstyle guitar played by Knopfler adds to the song's emotional impact, evoking feelings of introspection and longing. The lyrics, which highlight the effects of war on people and their relationships, strike a deep chord with listeners. A defining characteristic of Knopfler's work, this deep storytelling skill distinguishes him as a superb lyricist.

Other songs on the CD highlight Knopfler's depth and skill as a songwriter. One of Dire Straits' most well-known songs is "Money for Nothing," a reflection on the music business and rock stars' lifestyle that uses clever language and an appealing hook. The song's iconic opening guitar riff, developed through a unique guitar effect, not only defined the era's sound but also showcased Knopfler's inventive approach to guitar playing. Its place in music history was further cemented when it received a lot of exposure and was awarded the Grammy Award for Best Rock Performance by a Duo or Group.

Another noteworthy song, "Walk of Life," has a more joyful and festive tone and demonstrates Knopfler's talent for creating catchy melodies. The song's piano-driven composition and sing-along chorus made it a favorite among fans and a staple of live performances. The album "Walk of Life" was widely popular because of Knopfler's ability to integrate many musical genres.

He did this by skilfully combining rock with parts of country and folk.

Beyond the album's greatest successes, the more introspective tunes showcase Knopfler's sophisticated storytelling skills. Songs like "Your Latest Trick" and "So Far Away" offer a window into his perceptions and experiences. The former evokes a sense of desire and remoteness, while the latter provides a vivid picture of a momentary romantic encounter. Knopfler creates a connection with his audience that lasts long after the music stops by bringing them into his universe through vivid imagery and intense emotional depth.

Beyond its short-term success, "Brothers in Arms" left a lasting legacy by inspiring other musicians and songwriters in various genres. Its themes of violence and humanity continue to be necessary, stimulating discussions about combat and its implications. Musicians have been influenced by the album's elaborate arrangements and luxurious production to experiment with comparable soundscapes and include narrative into their compositions. Many different types of artists credit Knopfler as an influence, pointing out that his skill at telling stories via music has influenced their songwriting.

Furthermore, "Brothers in Arms" has endured in popular culture thanks to its incorporation into documentaries, TV series, and movies. Its continuing appeal can be ascribed to the universal issues portrayed in Knopfler's lyrics, which resonate with audiences regardless of time or place. For example, the title track has been utilized to show the human cost of war in various circumstances, illustrating the power of music to elicit strong emotions and mental processes.

Knopfler's songwriting prowess is not limited to "Brothers in Arms." Over his career, his ability to tell compelling stories has been a defining characteristic. From his early days with Dire Straits to his solo endeavors, Knopfler has steadfastly dedicated himself to relevant and intimate storytelling. His compositions frequently incorporate elements of fantasy and truth, drawing from his personal experiences to encourage listeners to consider their own lives.

CHAPTER 6: A SOLO CAREER OF ARTISTIC FREEDOM

Transitioning from Dire Straits to a solo career

Mark Knopfler had to make a big career decision when he went solo after Dire Straits' enormous success. After the band's last studio album, *On Every Street*, came out in 1991, Knopfler decided to pull back from the spotlight of being a rock star. After Dire Straits formally dissolved, he was left to consider his next steps as a musician and how to forge a new identity outside of the band's pre existing structure.

Early in the 1990s, Knopfler started to develop his solo career as he looked to experiment with other musical genres and subjects that had seemed a little restricted during his time with Dire Straits. His debut solo album, *Golden Heart*, was widely praised when it was released in 1996 and represented a significant shift from the sound that had made Dire Straits famous. While showcasing Knopfler's trademark fingerpicking guitar approach, the album also incorporated folk rock and Celtic music elements, among other inspirations. Songs like "Darling Pretty" and "Cleaning My Gun " demonstrated his development as an artist," which showed a more reflective and intimate approach to songwriting.

This was not just a change in musical taste but also a change in viewpoint. Being a solo artist allowed Knopfler to work with various musicians and try out new genres. His later recordings, on which he included elements of blues, country, and even traditional British folk music, demonstrate this experimentation. He explored his songwriting to a greater extent with each effort, producing rich, story-driven songs that appealed to both new and returning listeners.

With the release of *Sailing to Philadelphia* In 2000, Knopfler solidified his solo career and showcased his range as a musician. The album spawned successes like the title tracks "Sailing to Philadelphia" and "What It Is," it featured collaborations with well-known musicians like Van Morrison and James Taylor. These songs showcased his unique ability to merge storytelling with melodic expertise, and they rapidly became favorites among his fans. In addition to establishing his reputation as a solo performer, the album demonstrated his abilities as a songwriter who could produce classic songs without the influence of Dire Straits.

Knopfler continued to release highly regarded albums in the early 2000s, such as *Get Lucky* (2009) and *Privateering* (2012). With each album, he demonstrated his artistic development while retaining the unique guitar style and profound lyrics that his fans had grown to adore. His growth as a songwriter was evident in the songs from these albums, which frequently tackled topics of life, love, and the human experience. Songs like "Cleaning My Gun" and "Get Lucky" demonstrated his talent for engaging listeners in vivid tales with a global yet personal feel.

With his shift to a solo career, Knopfler was also able to work on several joint ventures, including film compositions and musical partnerships. His cinematic instincts had already been demonstrated by his work on movie soundtracks, such as the score for *Local Hero* (1983), but as a solo artist, he took full advantage of these changes. He also proved his ability to write emotionally charged music beyond conventional songwriting bounds with his scores for films such as *The Princess Bride* (1987) and *Wag the Dog* (1997).

Notable albums and collaborations that shaped his post-band career

Many noteworthy albums and collaborations that have impacted Mark Knopfler's musical legacy have marked his post-Dire Straits career. Knopfler's solo work, which embraces various styles and genres, has reinforced his identity as a great storyteller through music while showcasing his progress as an artist.

Notable Albums

Golden Heart (1996)

Mark Knopfler's debut solo record, Golden Heart, significantly altered the sound of Dire Straits. With it, he delved into love, grief, and introspection themes, crafting a wonderfully nuanced musical environment. The album included hits like "Cleaning My Gun," which showcased his trademark fingerstyle guitar technique, and "Darling Pretty," which quickly became a radio favorite. The song's lyrics demonstrated Knopfler's storytelling prowess and established the tone for his following solo projects.

Sailing to Philadelphia(2000)

Knopfler's solo career took a significant turn with this album, which included collaborations with musicians like Van Morrison and James Taylor. The title piece, "Sailing to Philadelphia," relates the story of two historical figures—Charles Mason and Jeremiah Dixon—who delineated the border between Pennsylvania and Maryland. The album combined folk, rock, and country influences with Knopfler's distinct lyrical storytelling approach and was warmly appreciated. Songs like "What It Is" and "Cleaning My Gun" demonstrated his capacity to relate intimate stories to more general issues.

Get Lucky (2009)

Knopfler demonstrated his flexibility as a musician in "Get Lucky," fusing country and blues music elements. Several noteworthy pieces from the album, such as "Get Lucky" and "So Far from the Clyde," showcase his skill as a storyteller. The album's musicianship and production value were lauded by critics, who noted Knopfler's rich vocal delivery and fingerpicking technique. The album strengthened his reputation as a lone artist who could musically encapsulate life's experiences.

Privateering (2012)

This double CD, a noteworthy accomplishment in Knopfler's record, had various tracks demonstrating his ongoing songwriting development. In songs like "Redbud Tree" and "Haul Away," Knopfler tackled themes of love, longing, and time passing. The album was well-received by critics for its complexity and diversity, demonstrating his ability to blend disparate musical inspirations into a coherent whole. Privateering enhanced Knopfler's standing as a gifted musician and storyteller.

Get Lucky (2009) and Tracker (2015)

Both albums demonstrated Knopfler's dedication to musical inventiveness and profound lyrics. "Tracker" gained notoriety for its rock, blues, and folk influences combined with introspective lyricism. Songs like "Long Cool Girl" and "Beryl" demonstrated his talent for engaging listeners with fascinating stories. Critics gave the CDs high marks, praising his musicianship and capacity to evoke strong feelings via song.

Down the Road Wherever (2018)

This album, which included songs that emphasized Knopfler's observations on life and love, represented another turning point in his solo career. Knopfler's humor and charm were evident in songs like "Good on You Son" and "My Bacon Roll," his ability to tell a good story resonated with his listeners. The album's varied sound, which featured jazz and rock influences, demonstrated Knopfler's versatility as a performer even further.

Notable Collaborations

Cinematic work

Knopfler has composed memorable music for films such as "The Princess Bride" (1987) and "Local Hero" (1983), among other prominent soundtracks. His writing talent was deeply felt, and his work in motion pictures demonstrated music that went beyond conventional songwriting. His distinctive guitar style and lyrical themes were frequently included in the soundtracks, which improved the films' narrative quality.

Collaborations with Other Artists

Over his solo career, Knopfler has worked with various musicians, which has expanded his artistic horizons. His collaborations on All the Roadrunning (2006) with Emmylou Harris and "The Last Laugh" with Van Morrison are prime examples of his ability to meld genres and produce ageless music. Through these partnerships, Knopfler has been able to take his music to a wider audience and explore new creative directions.

Live Performances and Tours

One of the most notable aspects of Knopfler's post-band career has been his live appearances. His ability to captivate audiences with both solo material and Dire Straits classics has cemented his image as an engaging performer. Notable tours that demonstrated his growth as a musician and drew enthusiastic audiences were Get Lucky and Privateering. Extended guitar solos, deft fingerpicking, and a mix of narratives that engage audiences personally are standard features of his live performances.

CHAPTER 7: COMPOSER FOR THE SILVER SCREEN

Knopfler's work in film scores, including "Local Hero" and "The Princess Bride"

In addition to showcasing his musical diversity, Mark Knopfler's venture into film scoring has considerably impacted the cinematic world. His compositions for *Local Hero* (1983) and *The Princess Bride* (1987) are two of his most well-known works. These works demonstrate Knopfler's capacity to produce compelling soundscapes that improve narrative, which makes him a highly sought-after composer in the motion picture business.

Local Hero (1983)

Bill Forsyth's endearing comedy-drama Local Hero is set in the made-up Scottish town of Ferness. The movie centers on Mac, an American oil executive (played by Peter Riegert), who is sent to work with an oil firm to negotiate the village's acquisition. As he becomes immersed in the native way of life, he starts to recognize the elegance and simplicity of village life.

Given Knopfler's increasing stature as a musician and songwriter—especially after Dire Straits' success—he was asked to write the score. "Local Hero"'s score is noteworthy for its unique fusion of rock and folk elements, which both nod to the Scottish location of the movie and maintain a distinctly Knopfler aesthetic. The film's whimsical and melancholy moments are complemented by the melodious yet subtle soundtrack created by his unique fingerpicking guitar approach.

The film's central theme, sometimes known as the "Local Hero Theme," is a soft, melodic tune that captures the story's spirit. Since then, it has become one of Knopfler's most well-known compositions. In addition to highlighting important moments, the music fosters emotional ties between the viewer and the characters. The music was well received by both reviewers and spectators for its ability to capture the atmosphere and scenery of Scotland and successfully transport listeners to the movie's setting.

Knopfler's debut as a film composer was primarily attributed to his work on Local Hero. Over time, the picture developed a cult following thanks to its long memory, critical success, and unforgettable score. With this project's help, Knopfler could show off his skills outside the concert hall and investigate additional film-scoring opportunities.

The Princess Bride (1987)

Four years after "Local Hero," Knopfler received an invitation to write the soundtrack for Rob Reiner's "The Princess Bride," a fantasy adventure classic based on William Goldman's book. The plot follows Westley on his quest to save Buttercup, his true love, and combines humor, romance, and adventure.

The tone of Knopfler's music for The Princess Bride is whimsical and adventurous, perfectly capturing the movie's storyline. The soundtrack combines acoustic guitar with orchestral arrangements to highlight Knopfler's distinctive sound and add elements that accentuate the fantasy aspects of the film. The story's emotional and humorous parts are reflected in the sound design, which is enhanced by the mandolin and other instruments.

Westley and Buttercup's romance is encapsulated in the "Storybook Love" theme, one of the score's most notable compositions. The film's fairy tale feel is echoed by the lovely and nostalgic melody that lingers throughout. Knopfler wrote the song "Storybook Love," which plays during the film's closing credits in addition to the instrumental score, adding to the music's emotional impact.

The score that Knopfler composed for the movie was praised by critics for feeling both classic and essential to the narrative. His contributions to "The Princess Bride" not only improved the experience for the audience but also added to the whimsical appeal of the movie, solidifying its place in history as a treasured classic. Over time, the music has maintained its appeal and been praised for its capacity to bring back the movie's most memorable scenes.

Mark Knopfler's contributions to movie soundtracks have proven his ability to fuse music and narrative. His soundtracks have the power to evoke feelings and memories long after the credits have rolled, as demonstrated by "Local Hero" and "The Princess Bride". With his unique blend of cinematic storytelling and guitar, Mark Knopfler has carved out a special place for himself in film music.

How cinematic composition deepened his musical expression

Mark Knopfler's research of cinematic composition has deeply broadened his musical expression, allowing him to expand his artistic boundaries beyond the usual confines of rock music. As a musician, he has always been known for his storytelling skills. Still, his film scoring work has helped him build a fuller narrative approach that integrates musical and cinematic components.

With the help of films like "Local Hero" and "The Princess Bride", Knopfler started composing music for motion pictures, realizing the special effect music can have on telling a story. This encounter changed how he approached songwriting and composition, encouraging him to consider more carefully how music may accentuate visual storytelling and arouse particular feelings. Making music for film demanded a different kind of thinking; instead of writing songs to be played live, Knopfler had to create soundscapes that blended in perfectly with the stories, people, and images in the movies.

His drive to adapt music to the emotional tone of a scene drove him to hone his craft. For example, he started to use more nuanced dynamics, building tension and atmosphere with quiet and white space. This contrasts his early Dire Straits career when he was recognized for more straightforward rock arrangements. He learned the value of timing from composing for movies, and he started using pauses and rhythmic changes to enhance the emotional effect of his songs.

Knopfler widened his sound palette and added more instruments to his cinematic works, enhancing the intricacy of his musical interpretation. Together with his distinctive electric and acoustic guitars, he used a range of instruments, such as strings, woodwinds, and diverse percussion parts. This research enhanced his sound, enabling him to produce more layers and atmosphere in his songs.

For instance, Knopfler used the accordion and mandolin in the soundtrack of "The Princess Bride" to create an air of whimsical adventure. These selections mirrored the movie's storyline and gave the music a distinct personality that conventional rock arrangements might not have been able to accomplish. Knopfler's approach became recognizable for combining disparate sounds into a unified whole, distinguishing him from his peers.

Knopfler's more profound connection to storytelling due to his film work is one of the most important effects on his talent. After discovering cinematic composing, he started to consider his music as an essential component of a story rather than just a stand-alone piece. This transition allowed him to compose songs that expressed a plot arc, character development, and emotional journeys, frequently reflecting the themes and moods presented in the films.

In his later solo work, this influence is evident in songs like "Cleaning My Gun" and "Get Lucky," where the storylines weave complicated tales filled with imagery and emotion. He appreciates how music can alter perception and improve narrative, which is evident in his ability to create rich musical landscapes that connect with listeners on a deeper level.

The cinematic composing techniques Knopfler developed have had a noticeable impact on his live performances. By adding additional story-driven songs to his setlists, he adopted a storyteller's mindset for live performances, engrossing audiences in the legends that accompanied his songs. Every performance is a different journey because of the immersive experience he was able to create for the audience through the use of dynamic arrangements and various instrumentation.

Extended instrumental passages are a standard part of his concert performances, allowing him to express himself musically and emotionally without using words. This strategy is similar to his storytelling methods in movies, where the music may elicit emotions and convey meaning. With his concerts being more of a narrative experience, Knopfler's development as a performer has allowed listeners to engage with the music on a deeper level.

CHAPTER 8: COLLABORATIONS WITH LEGENDS

Working with artists like Bob Dylan, Eric Clapton, and Emmylou Harris

Mark Knopfler has worked with some of the greatest names in music throughout his storied career, such as Emmylou Harris, Eric Clapton, and Bob Dylan. These collaborations show off his flexibility as a musician and his capacity to meld his sound with a wide range of other musicians' inspirations.

Collaboration with Bob Dylan

One of Knopfler's most well-known collaborations was with the renowned rock and folk musician Bob Dylan.

On Dylan's 1986 album "Infidels", Knopfler performed on guitar. His subtle yet distinctive fingerpicking gave the record a new depth, which went well with Dylan's lyrics. Dylan's eloquent storytelling and the album's overall mood were enhanced by Knopfler's melodic contributions to songs like "Jokerman" and "I and I."

Following "Infidels", their cooperation persisted. Knopfler also toured with Dylan in 1987 to promote the record. This was an even more significant creative leap for him, sharing the stage with one of his favorite musicians. The live performances won praise for their seamless interplay between Dylan's introspective lyrics and Knopfler's skillful guitar playing, enthralling audiences.

Working with Eric Clapton

The collaboration between Eric Clapton, another guitar legend, and Knopfler has resulted in some fantastic musical moments. In 1990, Knopfler played guitar on

Clapton's Journeyman album. His rendition of "Tearing Us Apart" showcased his compatibility with Clapton's unique blues style. The two guitarists worked well together, combining their individual styles to create a unified sound that delighted fans of both musicians.

Knopfler and Clapton cooperated in live performances, sharing the stage at numerous charity events, like the renowned 1999 Concert for the Rainforest Foundation. Their joint efforts highlighted their music's emotional depth while showcasing their technical skill. Together, they performed impassioned renditions of well-known songs, with Clapton's bluesy riffs and Knopfler's fingerpicking blending together beautifully to create an electrifying atmosphere that left fans speechless.

Collaborating with Emmylou Harris

Mark Knopfler's collaboration with renowned country and folk vocalist Emmylou Harris represents another significant phase in their artistic journey. Their creative connection was fully displayed on her 2008 album *All I Intended to Be*, which Knopfler produced and played on. The record combines rock, folk, and country influences, and Knopfler's guitar work perfectly balances Harris's heartfelt vocals.

One standout song on the album is "Beyond the Blue," where Harris's poignant performance is complemented by Knopfler's masterful fingerstyle guitar, creating an ethereal and depressing atmosphere. The partnership demonstrates the ability of both musicians to include narratives in their songs, and their combined skills produce a deep, complex sound that appeals to listeners.

They stayed together even outside of the studio as Knopfler toured with Harris. These live performances demonstrated their deep musical connection and the seamless way their instrumentation and voices blended to provide audiences with a fantastic experience. Knopfler's adaptability and desire to experiment with different musical settings are further demonstrated by his ability to modify his style to fit Harris's genre.

In addition to broadening Knopfler's musical horizons, his partnerships with Bob Dylan, Eric Clapton, and Emmylou Harris enabled him to explore a broader range of styles and genres. He was pushed to grow as a musician by playing with such well-known artists, who inspired him to experiment with sound and broaden his creative boundaries.

How these collaborations influenced his musical evolution

Mark Knopfler's musical career, talent, and creative possibilities have been greatly enhanced and shaped by his partnerships with iconic musicians such as Eric Clapton, Bob Dylan, and Emmylou Harris. With the distinct influences each partnership offered, Knopfler was able to experiment with various styles, methods, and approaches to narrative.

He became acquainted with the nuances of narrative-driven songwriting and lyrical profundity through his collaboration with Bob Dylan. Dylan's ability to craft songs that evoke strong feelings and cover political and emotional subjects inspired Knopfler to delve deeper into the craft of songwriting. Not only does this demonstrate Knopfler's technical proficiency, but working with "Infidels" on guitars also led him to think about how music could improve and elevate storytelling. His approach to composition changed significantly due to this collaboration, as he was forced to concentrate on how his guitar playing could heighten the words' emotional impact.

Knopfler's repertoire gained a bluesier flavor due to his collaboration with Eric Clapton. Well-known for being a genre authority, Clapton urged Knopfler to try different guitar techniques and improvisational strategies. The two guitarists' ability to collaborate successfully resulted in performances that allowed them to share information and highlighted their distinctive tones. Through this cooperation, Knopfler's fingerpicking technique was refined and became more expressive, using more blues-influenced licks than in his solo work.

By working with Emmylou Harris, Knopfler expanded his creative horizons by exploring folk and country music worlds. The combination of Harris's expressive voice and storytelling skills with Knopfler's sound created a complex blend of sounds that captivated listeners. Together, they created *All I Intended to Be*, which showed off his versatility as an artist by allowing him to modify his characteristic guitar work to suit the subtleties of many genres. Because of this partnership, Knopfler was inspired to write songs with a softer, more narrative style emphasizing the emotional bond between the song's lyrics and melody.

Together, these partnerships shaped Knopfler's musical development and allowed him to add a variety of components to his compositions. Working with such significant musicians and being exposed to other musical traditions encouraged Knopfler to be more experimental in his composing and performance. His latter albums reflect a blend of rock, blues, folk, and country influences, each presenting a layer of his musical journey formed by these experiences.

Moreover, the friendships and professional contacts developed via these collaborations provided Knopfler with a supportive network of artists who shared a passion for music. The ideas and experiences he shared with these idols enhanced his artistic perspective, and he was inspired to take creative chances. He was able to develop as a storyteller and musician in this supportive atmosphere, which helped him write songs that are both intensely personal and incredibly relatable to everyone.

These encounters gave Knopfler a distinctive sound that transcends genres and reflects the various influences he has collaborated with. His ability to mix exquisite guitar melodies with profound storytelling has become a characteristic of his work, setting him apart in the industry. Knopfler's subsequent work bears the influence of Dylan's rich lyrics, Clapton's bluesy improvisation, and Harris's poignant emotional resonance, demonstrating the creative growth and inventiveness that can result from collaboration.

CHAPTER 9: THE GUITAR COLLECTOR AND ENTHUSIAST

Knopfler's love for vintage guitars and their role in his music

A key component of Mark Knopfler's musical persona, his passion for old guitars has shaped his sound and approach. Early in his career, he developed a fondness for vintage instruments, which he carried throughout his musical career. With a collection of some of the most recognizable guitars—each with a distinct history and personality—Knopfler can experiment with different tonal characteristics that influence his music.

Knopfler is quite proud of his 1958 Gibson Les Paul Standard, which he calls "Lucy." Thanks to its gorgeous design and deep, warm tones, this instrument has played a significant role in his sound, especially on older Dire Straits songs. Thanks to Les Paul's adaptability, he can easily transition between a strong, sustained lead tone and a softer, more melodic touch. This instrument displays the dynamic range that old guitars may provide to his music and illustrates his ability to merge folk, blues, and rock elements.

In addition, Knopfler is well-known for his love of Fender Stratocasters, especially the late 1960s and early 1970s models. His use of the Stratocaster adds to his distinctive fingerpicking style by producing a crisper, brighter sound that accentuates his deft playing techniques. Because of its ergonomic design, the Stratocaster is perfect for his distinct playing style, allowing him to explore intricate melodies and harmonies effortlessly. Songs like "Sultans of Swing" show how Strat's expressive sound and tonal clarity improve the storytelling in his songs, giving the lyrics a more vivid quality.

Beyond their aesthetic appeal, he appreciates the histories and personalities that each vintage guitar offers. Knopfler frequently discusses how these guitars inspire him creatively and link him to the musical traditions that have shaped him over the years. Vintage guitars have a patina that reflects the hands of innumerable musicians who have played them, giving them a depth and history that parallels Knopfler's musical journey.

Throughout his career, Knopfler has also worked with several luthiers to create guitars tailored explicitly to his playing style. His ability to keep his unique sound while embracing new musical endeavors results from his ability to meld vintage charm with contemporary expertise. His custom-built "Fender Telecaster" and other instruments have given him the ideal blend of old-world appeal and modern convenience, expanding his range of sounds even further.

The significance of vintage guitars in Knopfler's music is apparent in his live and studio performances. His careful attention to detail is evident in every concert, as he carefully chooses instruments that complement the songs' mood. This intentionality improves audiences' overall experience by enabling them to perceive the subtleties of his sound stemming from each guitar's distinctive characteristics.

Furthermore, Knopfler's commitment to maintaining vintage instruments reflects a wider admiration for the creativity and artistry of guitar creation. He has frequently underlined the value of respecting musical tradition and realizing how sound has changed. This attitude carries over into his music, as he skillfully blends elements from several genres and historical periods to create a rich auditory tapestry that captures his love of the guitar and his background.

Insights into his most cherished instruments

Mark Knopfler has a special bond with his guitars, which are more than just musical instruments in his hands. Each guitar has a unique history and meaning. He frequently expresses gratitude for the guitars that have supported him throughout his career, sharing details about why particular instruments are particularly dear to him and how they help to define his unique sound.

One of Knopfler's most treasured instruments is his 1958 Gibson Les Paul Standard, renowned for being called "Lucy." This guitar has evolved into more than just a vintage guitar; it now plays a significant role in his musical identity. Knopfler has described Lucy as having an unmatched warmth and depth in tone. The guitar's rich history—having been played by various musicians before him—adds to its allure. He enjoys the character that age lends to the instrument, noticing how the wood settles and the pickups respond differently over time. Some of his most well-known songs feature Lucy's strong sound, proving that the right instrument can improve a song.

Knopfler also cherishes his Fender Stratocaster as an instrument. He has multiple Stratocasters, especially the late '60s and early '70s models, which he believes are necessary to play in his distinctive fingerpicking technique. Knopfler is impressed by the Strat's clear, bright tone, which enables him to convey complex melodies. He frequently selects different Stratocasters for different performances, choosing them according to their distinct tonal characteristics and how well they fit particular tunes. His careful choice of instruments demonstrates his profound appreciation of how a guitar's intricacies may heighten the emotional effect of music.

In addition, Knopfler has a particular fondness for his Telecaster, which he frequently credits as an essential component of his sound. The Telecaster, well-known for its clarity and twang, adds a unique sharpness that complements his storytelling approach. He has talked about how the Telecaster fits nicely in his hands and enables him to play with an accuracy that he enjoys. This guitar has greatly influenced Dire Straits' sound, especially on songs like "Telegraph Road," whose distinct tone gives the song a more profound, resonant quality.

Apart from these recognizable models, Knopfler has also worked with luthiers to design unique instruments that fit his playing style. These custom guitars frequently blend contemporary features with vintage aesthetics, allowing him to play instruments that fulfill his unique performance requirements while preserving the classic sound he adores. He likes to play around with these custom designs, frequently looking for unusual pickups and woods with distinctive tones. Every project involving a luthier represents his continuous pursuit of the ideal sound and the production of a new instrument.

Knopfler's insights into his cherished instruments demonstrate his tremendous admiration for craftsmanship and the creativity involved in guitar-making. He knows that every guitar has a story to tell and conveys the spirit of the music that is played on it. This reverence extends to the history of each instrument, acknowledging the hands who played them before and the journey they have taken. He frequently states that the best guitars resonate with him sonically and emotionally, indicating that they are essential to his creative process.

Beyond the technical details, Knopfler has a very intimate relationship with his instruments. He frequently talks about how playing a particular instrument has inspired him, how it has influenced his songwriting, or how it felt during a memorable performance. Every guitar is a comrade to him; they have shared many musical achievements and seen him grow as an artist.

CHAPTER 10: BEYOND THE STAGE – MARK KNOPFLER'S PERSONAL JOURNEY

Life outside of music: passions, philanthropy, and personal growth

Mark Knopfler is multifaceted and goes beyond his identity as a guitarist and songwriter. His life away from music is a rich tapestry of passions, philanthropy, and personal development. Even while his musical contributions have made him well-known, his activities off stage demonstrate a solid dedication to various causes and a sincere appreciation for life's wide range of experiences.

He has a strong interest in books. He reads a lot and frequently loses himself in books that examine human connections, history, and the complexities of life. His appreciation of narrative enhances his songwriting and broadens his perspective on the world. He was influenced by writers like Ernest Hemingway and Gabriel García Márquez, which gave his lyrics a more profound sense of narrative. Knopfler's love of literature is evident from how he creates rich narratives in his songs, engaging listeners in vibrant settings that mirror his literary sources.

Knopfler has a deep respect for films in addition to books. He frequently discusses how movies have inspired his songwriting and creative process. His work on film scores, including "Local Hero" and "The Princess Bride," exemplifies his ability to create emotionally charged music that complements visual storytelling. In addition to his work as a composer, Knopfler likes to watch various films, from classics to new releases. His love of stories that explore human emotions and relationships, in particular, has strengthened his conviction in the potency of narrative, whether it be through song or film.

Beyond music, philanthropy plays a significant role in Knopfler's life. He has participated in many charitable activities and frequently uses his position to advocate for causes that he finds necessary. For example, he has contributed to organizations that support music education, guaranteeing that the transforming effect of music is available to future generations. Knopfler acknowledges the value of supporting emerging talent and has participated in programs that give aspiring musicians tools and opportunities. His dedication to philanthropy reflects his values of encouraging people's creativity and giving back to the community.

Knopfler has also demonstrated support for environmental causes. He has participated in initiatives to advance sustainability and is aware of the effects of climate change. He exhibits a sense of responsibility towards the world by promoting awareness and action, connecting his principles with a dedication to preserving the environment for the coming generations. This enthusiasm for conservation is an extension of his artistic sensibilities, as he often gets inspiration from the natural world, reflected in the images within his lyrics.

One recurrent topic in Knopfler's life is personal development. He has embraced the concept of lifelong learning and is constantly looking for new opportunities to broaden his horizons and develop. This development may be heard in his music and in how he views relationships, life, and the arts. He appreciates the life experiences of becoming older, realizing how they mold his worldview and foster his creativity. His personal life is enhanced, and he stays relevant in the ever-evolving music industry thanks to his openness to learning and adapting.

Knopfler appreciates the small pleasures in life and likes to spend time with friends and family when he has free time. He cherishes the relationships he has built over the years and frequently finds inspiration and comfort in the ones most important to him. These experiences enhance his general well-being and influence his artistic expression, whether they involve telling stories over a meal or traveling to new locations. He understands the value of maintaining a healthy balance in his life and ensuring that his relationships and activities outside of work are just as fulfilling as his career pursuits.

The Legacy of a Guitar Genius

Mark Knopfler's legacy as a guitar wizard is a fantastic tapestry from his creative methods, unique sound, and profound impact on countless musicians. Knopfler has reinvented the art of guitar playing and made an enduring imprint on rock music, from his early days with Dire Straits to his successful solo career.

He left behind a unique style of fingerpicking that is unmatched in the music industry. In contrast to many guitarists who use a pick, Knopfler evolved a technique that allows him to pluck the strings with his fingertips, giving his performance a unique sensitivity and nuance. With this technique, he can create a broad range of tones and dynamics, giving his music a richness and warmth that appeals to listeners. His seamless fusion of rhythm and melody has encouraged many guitarists to explore fingerstyle playing, expanding the range of rock music's tonal possibilities.

His songwriting prowess is another cornerstone of his fame. His songs generally reflect rich storytelling, bringing listeners into fascinating scenarios exploring love, sorrow, and human experience. Songs like "Sultans of Swing" and "Brothers in Arms" illustrate his aptitude for weaving familiar yet significant stories. His ability to narrate stories not only improves his songs but also links listeners and his work's emotional depth. Because of this, many modern songwriters credit Knopfler as having significantly influenced them, mentioning how his lyrical style influenced their work.

Knopfler's guitar sound has become recognizable with its clear, expressive tone. This distinctive sound is influenced by his usage of old instruments, especially his cherished Fender Stratocaster. This guitar is typically connected with the rich, clear notes and the characteristic twang that have become hallmarks of his playing. Knopfler's legacy encourages musicians to further investigate the relationship between instrument and sound. His selections of gear reflect his profound appreciation for the trade.

His influence also goes beyond the records he has released. His work as a producer and collaborator has produced remarkable productions that exhibit his versatility and grasp of numerous musical forms. Working with well-known musicians like Bob Dylan, Eric Clapton, and Emmylou Harris, he contributed to improving their music with his skilled guitar playing and production knowledge. These partnerships demonstrate Knopfler's receptivity to various influences and emphasize his leadership role in the larger music scene, where he encourages originality and creativity.

He has also had a strong influence on movie soundtracks. His compositions for films such as "The Princess Bride" and "Local Hero" have won praise from critics, demonstrating his talent for writing music that harmonizes flawlessly with visual narratives. These soundtracks demonstrate his ability to craft moods and feelings that elevate the cinematic experience, demonstrating his versatility outside the genre of classic rock music. He has established himself as a versatile composer and musician by effectively crossing the realms of film and music.

One cannot exaggerate Knopfler's musical influence on the world stage. With albums like "Brothers in Arms" becoming bestsellers and influencing other artists worldwide, Dire Straits enjoyed enormous economic success. The group's ability to meld jazz, folk, and rock elements struck a chord with listeners worldwide, proving how popular Knopfler's skill is everywhere. His songs are still relevant to new audiences decades after they were initially released, demonstrating the enduring appeal of his work.

Knopfler's reputation has been cemented not just by his musical accomplishments but also by his honesty and sincerity as an artist. He is renowned for his modesty, commitment to work, and unwavering belief in his creative vision. Many musicians have prioritized their artistic integrity due to this unwavering commitment to quality, which supports the notion that true artistry demands passion and dedication.

CONCLUSION

Strings That Will Echo Forever

This examination of Mark Knopfler's life and career thus far clearly shows that he has made significant and enduring contributions to the music industry. Knopfler's talent is more than technical proficiency; it is a distinct voice that appeals to all age groups. His unique style of fingerpicking and melodic phrasing on the guitar has made him a rock star and encouraged many other musicians to explore the subtleties of their own instruments.

Knopfler has captured listeners with his storytelling talent through his songs, transforming ordinary situations into gripping tales. His songs frequently touch on common themes of human existence, allowing listeners to connect emotionally. His lyrical depth enlivens the musical landscape, elevating each song to timeless art, whether telling tales of love and loss or capturing the essence of everyday life.

Moreover, his eagerness to explore and engage with varied artists indicates a commitment to artistic inquiry that continues to affect the business. Through his collaborations with music icons such as Eric Clapton and Bob Dylan and his cinematic compositions, Knopfler has proven his versatility, keeping his music current and appealing to both new and devoted audiences.

Along with his artistic achievements, Knopfler's love of old instruments and equipment demonstrates his sincere passion for the trade, reminding him that creativity is about the process as much as the final product. His assortment of instruments, each with a unique history and personality, has been instrumental in creating his characteristic sound, confirming the notion that an artist's instruments significantly impact their artistic expression.

Upon contemplating Knopfler's legacy, it becomes evident that his influence surpasses just his critically acclaimed albums and number-one hits. His melodies reverberate in listeners' hearts long after the last note fades, making his music the soundtrack to many lives. Throughout his career, Knopfler has plucked strings that have resonated and woven a rich tapestry of sound that will inspire musicians of future generations.

Mark Knopfler's voyage is proof of music's ability to communicate and express oneself. We are reminded that the echoes of his strings will always exist as he creates and shares his talent with the world, encouraging us to listen, think, and discover our own stories within his created melodies. This guitar wizard's legacy is not just a mirror of his past; instead, it is a dynamic, living example of the music's eternal force that will encourage and inspire listeners for years to come.